Zombie Apocalypse

Mike Anderson

Copyright © 2013   Mike Anderson

All rights reserved. No part of this publication may be reproduced, distributed, or transmitted in any form or by any means, including photocopying, recording, or other electronic or mechanical methods, without the prior written permission of the publisher, except in the case of brief quotations embodied in critical reviews and certain other noncommercial uses permitted by copyright law.

Zombie Apocalypse

Table of Contents

Introduction 7
ZOMBIES: A BEGINNER'S GUIDE 11
ZOMBIE BEHAVIOR 23
BASICS OF SURVIVAL 29
WEAPONS 37
TRANSPORTATION 49
DEFENSE 61
WORST CASE SCENARIOS 67
Conclusion 73

Introduction

Zombies are probably the most popular monster in the world, and one of the reasons that they are so popular is that they are so much like us. Zombies are the ultimate apocalypse monster: every other horrible creature only threatens one or two people at a time, but zombies can wipe out the entire human race. There's a reason that there's no such thing as the "vampire apocalypse" or the "mummy apocalypse:" only zombies have the ability to grow into a giant hoard and destroy the earth as we know it.

It's fun to watch a zombie movie, or play a zombie video game. But a zombie outbreak can be really scary to be in…unless you know what to do. This book has been written to prepare you to survive. It is a collection of the most current and most effective zombie survival tactics and strategies available.

Sun Tzu, a great Chinese writer and general, once said "If you know the enemy and know yourself you need not fear the results of a hundred battles." This book is going to teach you everything you need to know about your enemy: zombies. Knowing about yourself is something you'll have to do on your own, but when you finish this book and start preparing, you might learn a thing or two about yourself, too.

This book was written with the collective teachings of many zombie survival experts, especially Max Brooks, author of "The Zombie Survival Guide." His teachings have already saved thousands, if not millions, of lives: this book will try to save a few more.

A zombie outbreak will often look something like this. You do not want to be any near this scenario.

ZOMBIES: A BEGINNER'S GUIDE

What is a Zombie?

Zombie movies don't usually explain what a zombie really is, or how they showed up. Hollywood cannot really be blamed for this, because even top scientists have only theories about the creation of zombies. However, we definitely know where the *idea* for zombies came from.

Zombies came from the African religion of Voodoo. Voodoo priests would sometimes kidnap people and try to turn them into mindless slaves. First, they would force their victim to breathe in a special poison, a powerful neurotoxin that would paralyze the subject and make them unconscious. Next, the priest would bury the victim alive in a shallow grave for 24 hours. After the full day had passed, the priest would dig the victim up.

Of course, 99% of victims would be dead. However, very rarely, a person would survive the ordeal. The survivors were probably the unlucky ones: the victim would be a hollow shell of a human being, with no memory of who they were, their family or loved ones, or even of their own free will. They would become staring, drooling, moaning idiots, who only knew how to obey the orders of their Voodoo master.

These slaves came to be called *nzambi*. When Western explorers discovered Voodoo and the existence of these poor creatures, they interpreted their name as "zombie."

So, the original Voodoo zombie has an easy origin to understand. But what about the other zombie, the movie-monster that threatens the existence of the entire human race? Where did that creature come from?

The most accepted theory is that a special virus creates zombies. This virus is incurable, cannot be vaccinated against, and is 100% lethal. In the early stages of infection, victims suffer from headaches, dizziness, fever, and muscle pains. This progresses into skin discoloration, total body weakness, intense fatigue, and ultimately to coma followed by death.

Then, within 24 hours of death, the patient's body reanimates itself, but any human memory or soul is completely overwhelmed by a hunger for brains. The person has turned into a zombie, and will tirelessly chase and devour any human that it can catch.

ZOMBIE PHYSIOLOGY

Physiology is the study of the physical body of a creature: in this case, the zombie.

First of all, zombies aren't alive. A zombie is a reanimated body, but the body is dead. A zombie's heart does not beat. A zombie's blood is a dry, spongy paste. A zombie can use its lungs, but it does not need oxygen to move or eat. In fact, zombies don't need to eat at all: being dead, they don't use energy.

If it is a virus that creates zombies, then that virus is responsible for everything that the zombie does. Somehow, the virus is able to use the decaying muscle and skeleton of its host to seek out human prey. So, the most likely reason that zombies feed is not to provide nutrients, but to spread the virus and allow it to reproduce. Zombies are a method of reproduction for a virus.

The virus spreads by being transported into a fresh human through the bite of a zombie. Infection can also occur through exposure to zombie flesh and blood, particularly fresh zombie's blood that is still liquid and under pressure.

In some rare cases, the virus is actually airborne, but is not itself fatal. Instead, the virus infects humans, and when the hosts die by any means, the virus reanimates the body.

As you can imagine, this sort of outbreak is very dangerous, because every dead human creates another zombie to increase the size of the hoard.

Zombie Anatomy

The zombie looks like a normal human being, and still obeys most of the limits of the normal human body. A zombie is not faster, stronger, or in any way "better" than the person it once was. However, zombies are also no longer bound by certain human weaknesses, particularly pain and exhaustion.

All of a zombie's organs no longer function in any useful way. The stomach holds flesh, food, and random objects, but after enough feeding the stomach will simply burst and send all the built-up material into the zombie's abdominal cavity. From there, further stuffing can burst the skin of the zombie's belly and cause all the rotten flesh to come tumbling out onto the ground.

Oddly, a zombie's lungs can still "breathe:" this is what allows the zombie to create is signature moan.

Zombies can still use the five senses of sight, hearing, taste, touch, and smell, at least until the respective organs rot away or are destroyed. Unlike humans, which rely on sight above any other sense, zombies do not focus on any one sense and instead use them all equally to catch their prey. This means that zombies will notice sounds and smells that humans would normally ignore.

Zombies share one more similarity with humans: their brain is still the most important part of their body. Just like the human brain, the zombie brain controls the zombie's movements and behavior. This fact is what allows a zombie to be "killed."

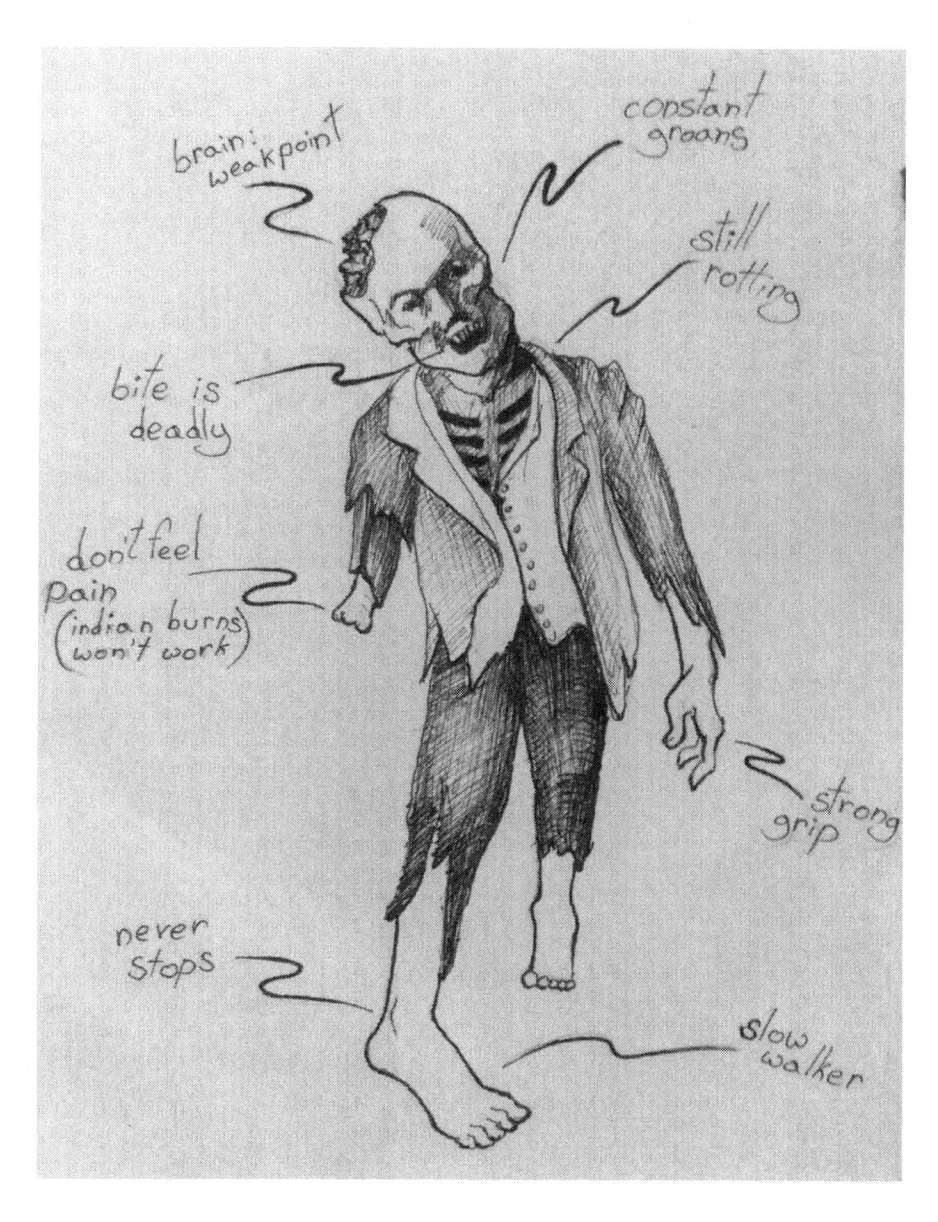

A student's infograph of a typical zombie. The note about indian burns seems silly, but it is important: you can only kill a zombie. You can never threaten or scare them.

Zombie Weaknesses

The zombie's reliance on the brain is its greatest weakness: if you destroy the brain, you also destroy the zombie. It doesn't matter how you destroy the brain. It can be crushed, smashed, sliced, burnt, splattered, or pureed. Whatever method is chosen, it must destroy the brain completely, or the zombie will continue to attack.

It is often believed that just cutting off a zombie's head is an effective way to kill the monster. This is wrong. It is true that a headless zombie's body will fall down and return to being a regular corpse. The zombie's head, however, will continue to snap, roll, and bite whatever it can reach. Sometimes you might have to decapitate a zombie in an emergency, but then the head should be destroyed as quickly as possible. More than one person has left a zombie head lying around, only to be bitten in the ankle.

Burning a zombie can kill it, but only if the fire destroys the zombie's brain. This can take a surprisingly long time: human bodies are not made to burn easily. While the zombie is burning, it will still freely and easily continue to stumble around trying to attack people. While it is doing so, it can light other things on fire. Sometimes it lights other zombies on fire, which is great, but most of the time it lights other stuff on fire. Like cities and forests.

Because fire is such an unreliable way to kill a zombie, it should only be used as a weapon of last resort, or as a way to kill large groups of disabled zombies all at once. For example, a nice bonfire can make quick work of a pile of several hundred snapping zombie heads.

Zombies have one more weakness: their nature as rotting human bodies. This rotting process is slowed, but not entirely stopped. The average zombie "lifespan" is 3-5 years, after which time the rotting will cause the zombie to literally fall apart. After a while, the skull will rot away, the brain will fall out, and the zombie will die.

Zombie Strengths

The obvious strength of the zombie is that unless the brain is destroyed, the zombie is unkillable. A zombie cannot be shot, stabbed, electrocuted, beaten, smothered, poisoned, crushed, or drowned. Therefore, killing a zombie is way harder than killing a human, and many effective human-to-human weapons are inefficient or completely pointless against a zombie.

Also, zombies do not feel pain. Weapons like tear gas, pepper spray, or rubber bullets hardly even slow zombies down. Only lethal force, applied to the head, can stop a zombie.

Zombie do not ever get tired. Humans get tired when their joints and muscles have been overused. Their bodies produce "fatigue toxins" that slow the body down and prevent the muscles from being used any more, to prevent serious long-term injuries. Zombies are not affected by these toxins anymore. This means that, while zombies do not have superhuman strength, their limitless endurance means that they can accomplish superhuman feats, given enough time. For example, a small group of zombies can eventually knock down a brick wall over weeks and months of attacking.

Thankfully, the fact that zombies do not get tired also means that they cannot heal. This is related to the zombie weakness of continuing to rot away: every time zombies attack, they destroy their muscles and bones. Zombies get weaker and weaker over time, while humans tend to get stronger and stronger as they push their limits. This means that a zombie is at its most dangerous when it first reanimates: during a zombie outbreak, be extremely careful around any and all dead bodies.

Understanding zombie anatomy is important because it shows you how to kill a zombie, but understanding zombie behavior can both keep you safe and give you the chance to kill one. The next section will go over what zombies do and don't do, and how to trick zombies for your benefit and survival.

ZOMBIE BEHAVIOR

<u>What Zombies Do</u>

Zombies are always hunting, or eating what they have hunted.

Zombies hunt by shambling about until their senses detect prey. Then, they home in on the prospect until they can make visual or physical contact. At that point, their jaws drop open, and they let out their terrifying, continuous moan. This moan gets louder and louder as the zombie gets closer and closer to prey, reaching its peak when the zombie grapples and bites its target.

Then, the zombie begins to eat. It always starts by gnawing through whatever limb or body part it got a hold of first. Next, it bites and claws at the head until the skull splits open, and then the zombie eats the brain. Finally, the zombie eats the flesh, bones, and organs.

Until the zombie eats the victim's brain, the zombie will not hunt anything else. Once the brain has been eaten, a zombie will stop feeding if it detects fresh prey nearby.

Once a zombie finds prey, the zombie will chase it until it loses all contact with the prey (i.e. it can no longer be seen, smelled, heard, or touched).

Scientists disagree about why zombies moan. Some see it as a fright tactic, meant to paralyze prey with fear, or panic it into running from cover. Others think it is a battle cry that brings other zombies in on the attack. A few think it the moan is just an accident, a pointless leftover from when the zombie was a human that could still think and speak.

Whatever the real reason, it is clear that the zombie moan DOES frighten people into panic or paralyses, and the zombie moan DOES attract other nearby zombies. That zombie moan is a dangerous weapon. Don't let a zombie see you, or it will use it.

What Zombies Don't Do

Zombies don't feel emotion, don't remember anything, and most importantly, don't think. Zombies are dumber than houseflies. They single-mindedly pursue prey, no matter the circumstances, and will walk right into any pit or trap in their way without slowing down.

Zombies never retreat. Zombies never show mercy. Zombies never give up.

Some people believe that zombies often return to their former places of work, or their homes, as if they have some tiny wisp of remaining humanity. This is not true: zombies do not have consciousness or self-identity. If zombies seem to appear where they once worked or lived, it's only because zombies tend to mill around where they were first infected until something makes them leave the area. Like chasing people.

Tricking a Zombie

Technically, it is impossible to trick or fool a zombie: something needs to have intelligence in order for it to be tricked. However, humans can use knowledge of zombie behavior to make them do stuff.

For example, when zombies are not actively chasing prey, noises like cracking twigs, footsteps, shouts, and gun shots attract zombie's attention and cause them to investigate the source of the noise. Therefore, zombies can be "lured" away from an area by using these kinds of noises to draw them on. These kinds of distractions are 100% successful as long as the zombie can sense them: a zombie will never consider that a suspicious noise is anything other than possible prey, and will always try to find the source.

On the other hand, attempting to distract a zombie that is already in "chase" mode is nearly impossible. Once a zombie has fixated on prey, the only thing that can get a zombie to change course is easier prey. This fact has led to many horrible situations where a group of humans, panicked and on the run from a hoard of zombies, hurts one member of the group and abandons them to die: the entire hoard attacks the helpless victim and forgets about the others.

Zombies always chase human prey when possible, but they will also catch and eat any other living animal. Humans have often had great success "luring" zombies by placing a wounded animal in a cage and hiding. The animal's cries attract zombies, which can then be picked off safely by the hiding humans. This strategy is cruel to animals, however, and in recognition of this some zombie "hunting parties" use one brave human as the bait. The bait is at extreme risk, especially if the zombies overwhelm the trap. The bait will, in this scenario, almost certainly be devoured before they can be helped.

The mention of "hunting parties" might make you start thinking about ways to exterminate a zombie outbreak. While eventually humans must attack the zombie menace, this is the last step after careful planning and preparation. Anyone who wishes to survive a zombie outbreak must first learn the basics of survival: against the environment, against zombies, and even against other humans.

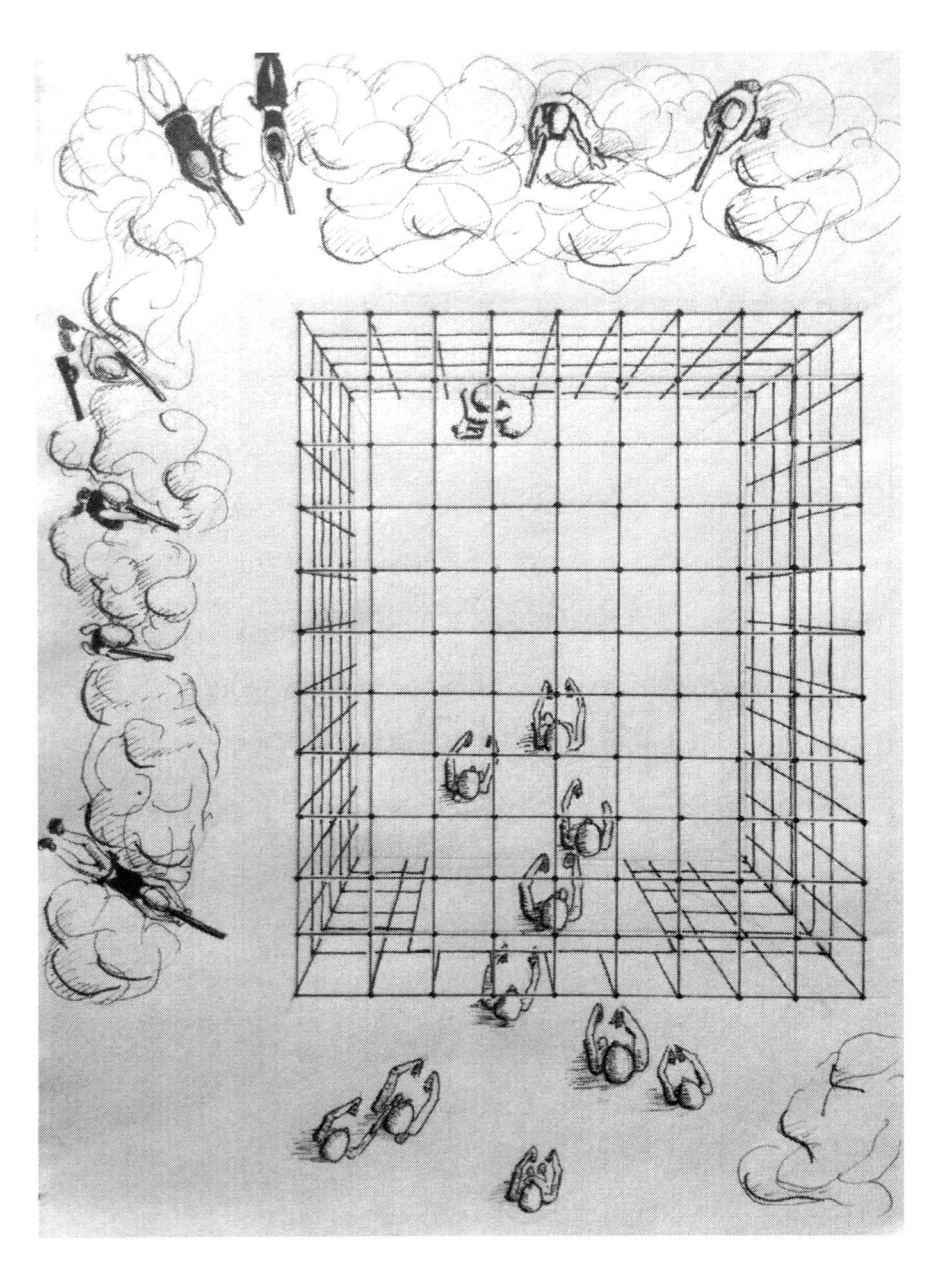

An example of a "trap" scenario going terribly wrong. Always make sure that your bait is securely locked inside.

BASICS OF SURVIVAL

Preparation for a Zombie Outbreak

During a zombie outbreak, many more people die from exposure, malnutrition, disease, and human violence than die from zombie attacks. In other words: people usually die from anything BUT zombies. Don't let that happen to you.

A human needs at least half a gallon of water, 1-2 pounds of nutritious food, 6-8 hours of sleep, warm clothing, and adequate shelter each day to survive. If you are planning to travel, double the amount of water and food you would need per day. Humans also need to have fun and spend time with other people to stay calm: just a few weeks without human contact or fun can drive sensitive people insane.

Humans also need adequate defenses. As a rule of thumb, every human in a given group needs to have one hand-to-hand weapon, one long or medium-range firearm, and a sidearm for emergencies, with about 50 rounds of ammunition for each. Ideas for the best guns and hand-to-hand weapons can be found in the chapter "weapons."

Finally, in case you forgot, humans need to be a part of a group. You're much better off fighting and surviving against zombies when you have other people to back you up. A group of humans can stand watches at night, gather more food and supplies, intimidate and ward off other groups, coordinate against zombie hoards, and dozens of other useful things.

However, a very large group can be inconvenient or even dangerous, especially in a crises situation like a zombie outbreak. A group should be 3-5 people, because small groups naturally stick together. If you have a good group, no one will argue about who the leader it, and people will just do what they have to do.

Before the zombie outbreak happens, you should have supplies prepared for at least a month, and ideally three months, of siege. This will allow you to carry 1-2 weeks worth of supplies for travel if and when you need to move. You should also know who will be in your group; how, where, and when your group will meet if an outbreak occurs; and who is responsible for what.

Finally, you must have a destination in mind. If you live in a city or town, then you will not be able to stay there if the outbreak is not contained by your government. You will need to have a fall-back destination, preferably someplace far away from humans. Prepare this spot ahead of time with plenty of supplies and gear.

Human Behavior During an Outbreak

It would be nice if every person had a zombie survival plan and conducted themselves in a smart way. Most people, however, are lazy and stupid. These kinds of people will, in a crises, either sit in their homes until the zombies devour them, or run screaming out into the streets or into their cars, where they will be killed by humans, accidents, or zombies.

These kinds of people account for 70-80% of the population. Any that aren't killed in the first few days will desperately try to reform the large groups and societies that they had before the zombie outbreak, and these groups will frequently experience fights, power struggles, and revolts.

There is a much smaller percentage of people who are much more dangerous. These people see a crises as an opportunity to take advantage of others, and can often be seen looting shops, attacking other people, throwing wild parties, and generally acting insane. These people often turn into bandits and raiders if an outbreak escalates too severely, and they are a danger to humans and zombies alike.

Then, finally, there are people like you: tough, honest folk who either know how to survive, or have an instinct for survival. They form into small bands and keep to themselves, helping others when possible, but never taking unnecessary risks. These small bands move and stop purposefully, and bandits and normal people rarely ever find them because they stay away from densely populated areas.

In the event of a worldwide zombie apocalypse, these small bands will eventually form new societies at the edges of the world, where there are few or no zombies.

Herds and Hoards

Humans naturally form groups, but zombies often appear in groups as well. These groups are entirely coincidences, because zombies seem to be aware of each-other the way they are aware of walls: they won't bump into them as often as they will walk around them.

A group of zombies about 5-20 members large is called a "herd." Herds are more dangerous than lone zombies because their numbers can overwhelm humans, and can more easily surround or corner them as well. When dealing with a herd of zombies, it is important to always maintain two escape routes at all times. Never let the zombies get behind you, or on both of your flanks. If you notice that zombies have gotten behind you, or are on either side and in front of you, run away towards the most open space available at a brisk jog. Do not ever sprint away from zombies, because you might accidentally run right into one, or trip and hurt yourself. Zombies move at a very slow pace, and so anything above a fast walk will quickly leave zombies in the dust.

Any group of zombies above 20 members is referred to as a "hoard." Hoards multiply the dangers of herds because they can swarm just about anything. Even a 20 foot tall concrete wall can be defeated by a hoard: the zombies will slowly pile on-top of each-other until they start to fall over the other side. Hoards also have a much easier time surrounding groups of humans.

Never, EVER try to run through, or attack, a hoard of zombies. Go around them, or turn around and try to find another route. If you have to attack a hoard for some reason, use lures to split the hoard into smaller herds. Splitting up your own group is never a good idea, if horror movies are any kind of example.

When Is It Time to Fight Back?

Going out to pick fights with zombies is a really bad idea. If there's a zombie outbreak and you're looking for some action, don't worry: the zombies will come to you. If you have a bunker or safe house, sit tight and kill zombies when you have to. If you're on the run, kill zombies that are chasing you.

Sooner or later though, you might have to go out into your neighborhood and exterminate zombies so that things can get back to normal. Don't go by yourself like an idiot: keep your group around, or at least have a buddy that will watch your back. Be smart about things like opening doors.

Cleaning a neighborhood out of zombies might seem like a great time to use fire. If you run around burning down everyone's houses so you can kill all the zombies though, then no one will have anywhere to live. Try to lure zombies out of the houses instead, and bring them down with guns. If you have to use fire, then you have to...but no one's going to thank you if you torch the whole block.

Speaking of guns and fire, it's time to talk about things that kill zombies: weapons.

WEAPONS

<u>What Makes a Good Weapon?</u>

A good weapon for fighting zombies needs to be reliable, simple to use, and consistently and quickly lethal to zombies. There are lots of other things to think about of course, but those three key points of reliability, simplicity, and lethality are the most important.

You should also think about the range of your weapon. The farther away a weapon can be used to kill a zombie, the better.

When it comes to reliability, simplicity, lethality, and range, guns rule. Although guns do require ammunition and are a little hard to take care of, no other weapon can kill so many zombies so safely.

Hand-to-hand weapons are important, but you should not try to "go berserker" and attack a herd of zombies with a fire axe. Hand-to-hand weapons are reliable, but they often require a fair amount of training to be used lethally, and they are slower to use against multiple attackers than a gun. So, you need a hand-to-hand weapon, but it can't be your only weapon or you're dead.

Nonlethal weapons are completely useless against zombies and should never be used in a zombie outbreak. These sorts of weapons include chemical sprays, soft-material bludgeons (like billy clubs), stun guns, and anything that can't deliver a solid, lethal blow to the head.

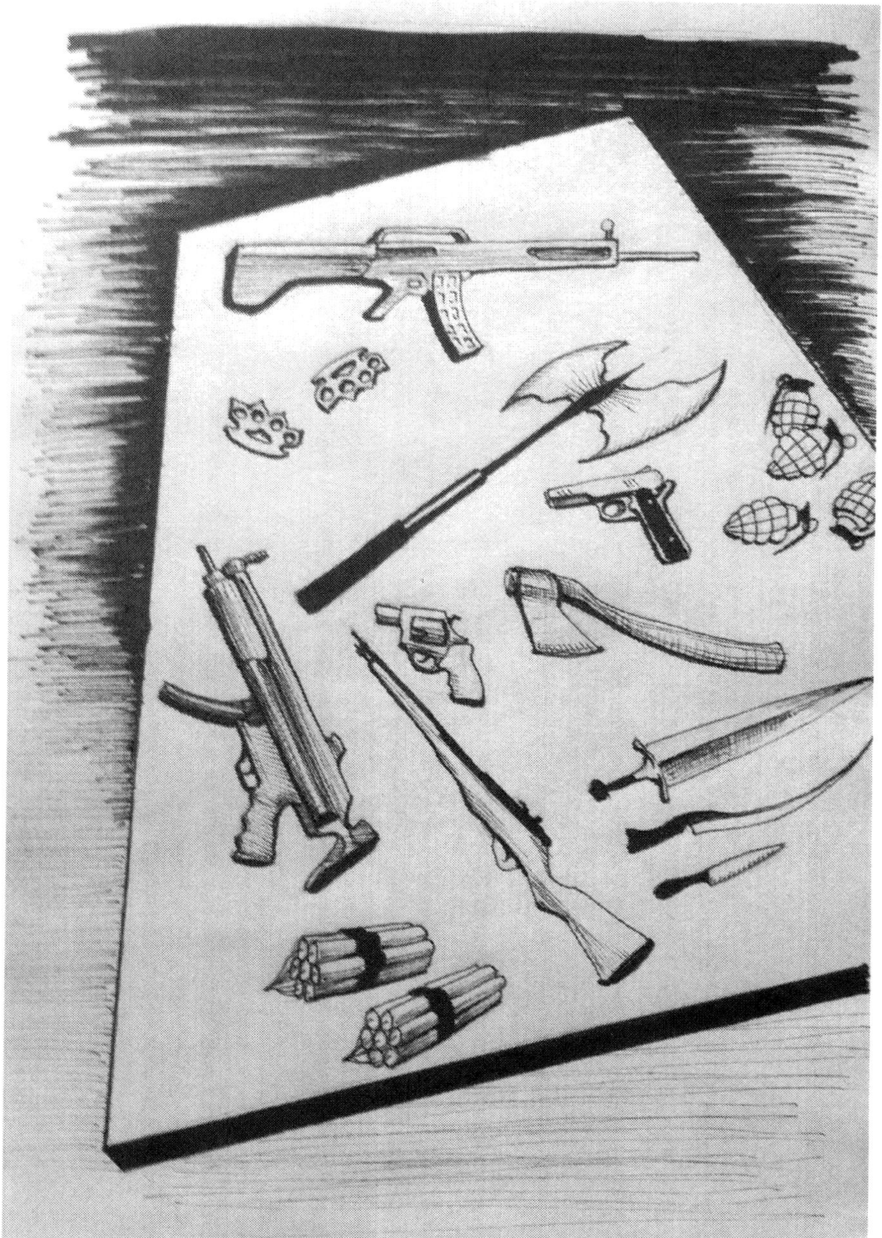

Guns

Guns are the best weapons for offense and defense against zombies for dozens of reasons. However, not all guns are created equal, and some guns that appear to be great zombie killing-machines are actually pretty bad.

For example, automatic weapons like assault rifles and machine guns make for bad zombie killers. Automatic fire is terrific for downing human targets, but they make an accurate attack to the head really hard. An average marksman can lay down a hundred rounds of automatic fire at a cluster of zombies and succeed in only killing five or so. Plus, finding ammo for a military weapon is not easy.

On the other hand, the simple bolt-action hunting rifle is considered by most experts to be the #1 zombie killing weapon available to the average person. These weapons are highly accurate, easy to use even by complete beginners, ammunition and maintenance supplies are widely available, and one shot to the head will kill a zombie over 99% of the time. The bolt-action system forces users to be careful with their shots, preventing wasted ammo and helping ensure that every bullet kills a zombie. A group of five humans with enough ammunition can make short work of a hoard of even 100 zombies in a matter of minutes if they use bolt-action rifles.

The shotgun has a reputation for being the classic zombie-killing gun, and it earns the reputation...mostly. It's true that a blast from a 12-guage will just about evaporate a zombie's head, but you need to be really close to a zombie for that to work, and being close to zombies is NOT what you should be trying to do. Shotguns also have a tough recoil that is hard for smaller people to handle.

Pistols are harder to use effectively than rifles and may not always be lethal. They are also much less accurate than other guns. On the other hand, when a zombie has grabbed you and its jaws are inches from your neck, nothing works better than a point-blank shot to the head with one of these sidearms. Always carry a pistol for emergencies, but take the word "sidearm" seriously.

Crossbows, while not technically guns, do the same thing: kill zombies from far away. Crossbows are lethal, easy to aim, and silent, which makes them great when you want to kill a zombie at a distance without attracting attention. However, finding ammo can be a little hard, and loading and caring for a crossbow often requires special training.

Hand-to-Hand Weapons

Hand-to-Hand weapons are used for slashing, stabbing, chopping, or bashing. Generally, chopping and bashing weapons are best for killing a zombie, while slashing weapons can be useful to decapitate in a pinch.

Slashing weapons include most swords, and king among them is the Japanese katana. The katana is considered to be the sharpest and toughest bladed weapon ever made. It can easily slice through bones and flesh. Cutting the head of a zombie in half is entirely possible with a katana, but even weak users can cut off a head. Make sure to kill the head afterwards.

European long swords can also be useful, but they are generally not as sharp as the katana, and therefore not as useful. Avoid super big swords, like the Scottish claymore, at all costs: they look cool, but they are tiring and hard to use.

Stabbing weapons like rapiers and foils might kill a zombie if they are stabbed through the temple or eye, but this kind of attack is very difficult. The World War II trench spike, on the other hand, is in a class by itself. It is a large spike attached to a hand-grip, and can be used to smash through a zombie's skull. Its shape makes it easy to remove and use again, making it a great weapon.

Chopping weapons are mostly axes. If you hit a zombie in the head with an axe, that zombie is dead. On the other hand, you might miss. Axes need a large swing to be effective, and missing can pull you off balance. In addition, axes have a bad habit of getting stuck in the skulls and bodies of the zombies that they hit, wasting precious time and possibly even getting you killed.

Finally, bashing weapons such as clubs, maces, and hammers have the advantages of never getting stuck and being the simplest of all weapons. Using them for lethal attacks takes a surprising amount of force: human skulls are very hard. Bashing weapons also can have the same problem that axes have, which is that a missed swing can throw the user off-balance.

Be careful when using any kind of hand-to-hand weapon, because they put you right next to the zombies you are trying to avoid. Never try to take on a group of zombies with a one-handed weapon: take down as few as possible to open an escape route, and get away.

Tools, Household Items, and Other Improvised Weapons

Although these are not meant to be weapons, somehow or another they will end up being used in a zombie outbreak.

A length of lead pipe works great for bashing for a while, but should be quickly replaced. This is because lead is too soft to hold its shape as a weapon for long, and after one or two skulls a lead pipe will be noticeably bent or even broken.

A heavy wooden baseball bat is a great weapon. Aluminum ones are light and can be swung faster, but they're not as heavy. This means that an aluminum bat won't kill a zombie very often, unless you've got a great homerun swing.

Clay flowerpots, frying pans, televisions, and other such things should be considered "single use" weapons. They can take out a single zombie in a pinch, but then the user is left with nothing. Don't bother carrying these kinds of weapons around, if possible.

The best improvised weapon is the good old fashioned crowbar. It is compact, lightweight, extremely durable, can deliver focused and lethal bashing attacks, and can be used for all sorts of things, like opening doors and boxes. In fact, crowbars are so useful you should consider it as your hand-to-hand weapon no matter what your options are, even if you have a katana. If a sword is not killing zombies, it isn't much use, but a crowbar can be useful in all kinds of situations.

Unarmed

The image of a karate master taking down hoards of zombies with his bare fists and feet sounds exciting and cool, but the reality is that it will almost never work. Zombies don't care much about bruises and concussions, so unless you have a punch that can shatter a skull, you should avoid attacking a zombie in unarmed combat. If you do have a punch that can shutter a skull, you're all set against zombies.

Joint locks are pointless against zombies for a lot of reasons. First of all, there is little or no point in incapacitating a zombie if you have to grab one and hold it to make that happen. Secondly, joint locks get half of their effectiveness by causing pain, but zombies will happily break their own arms to bite you. Lastly, a joint lock cannot kill a zombie.

However, any martial art that teaches defenses or escapes from grapples and holds can be life saving. In these cases, you will want to ignore any techniques that rely on inflicting pain to the attacker to make them loosen their grip: remember, zombies can't feel pain. You will want to learn skills that make grabbing more difficult or impossible, or throws that you can perform to shake a grappling zombie off of you.

If you have a bare-handed weapon, such as a set of knuckle-dusters, you might be able to kill a zombie with a good punch. However, if you had to choose between keeping brass knuckles on you, and keeping a pistol, which would you choose? The smart money is on the pistol. Whenever possible, stick to guns.

Fire and Explosives

Fire is awesome, but fire is dangerous. The fact is, a zombie on fire can do a lot more damage than a zombie not on fire.

This sad fact makes fire weapons, like the flamethrower, iffy to use. If one zombie on fire can cause mayhem, imagine what fifty zombies could do if someone lit them on fire with a flamethrower. Use fire to get rid of disabled zombies and zombie heads. That way, you can control the fire and guarantee that the zombies you burn actually burn. In these kinds of controlled situations, fire is terrific and should be used whenever possible.

Explosives like grenades, rockets, and landmines, should never be used at all. Explosives kill humans mostly by shredding them with shrapnel, and partially because the force of the explosion can cause the heart to stop. Therefore, unless a bit of shrapnel goes through a zombie's head, or the explosion rips the zombie to pieces, explosives are not great for zombie killing.

Whether you're exterminating zombies or running away to a safe zone, you need a way to get there. The next section talks about transportation.

TRANSPORTATION

Travel for Evasion vs. Travel for Attack

Travelling for evasion means you're trying to get from point A to point B as fast as you can. You want a vehicle that's fast and maneuverable.

Travelling for attack means you're trying to clean out zombies. You want a vehicle that's tough, and that can be used to turn zombies into road kill.

There are a few kinds of transportation you can use: cars, trucks, motorcycles, bikes, boats, airplanes, helicopters, and your own two feet. This section will help you pick the best option to get you out of a zombie zone alive, or kill every zombie in the area.

Cars and Trucks

Cars are absolutely everywhere. This is both their greatest strength and their greatest weakness.

On the one hand, a car is the easiest vehicle to find fuel for. A car is easy to operate, goes very fast, is big and heavy (which is great for running zombies over), and can help you carry lots more stuff than you and your group could ever otherwise carry.

But the biggest problem with cars is that everyone will immediately see these advantages in the event of an outbreak, and will try to escape using their cars right away. Thousands and thousands of panicked drivers will hit the roads and will likely create densely packed traffic that could extend in lines for miles and miles.

Some people will become trapped in these stampedes, and while they sit in their cars, the zombies will attack. For a zombie, a person trapped in a car is about the easiest prey possible. If you are going to use a car, make sure to stay off the main roads and highways.

Which leads to the other problem with cars: they're made to run on main roads and highways. Cars are terrific for use on smooth asphalt roads, but there aren't going to be a lot of those available in a zombie outbreak.

Finally, while fuel is easy to find for cars, this is only true for a little while. Over time, pumps will become empty or break. A car without gas is pretty much a giant steel box on wheels.

Trucks have all the problems that cars have, but multiplied. They're even less useful on uneven ground, use even more fuel, use a special kind of fuel, and are too big to maneuver.

But, a truck can be a castle on wheels. It provides high ground for your attackers, and its massive size can squash dozens of zombies without damaging the truck at all. Never pick a truck when running away...but consider using one if you need to exterminate.

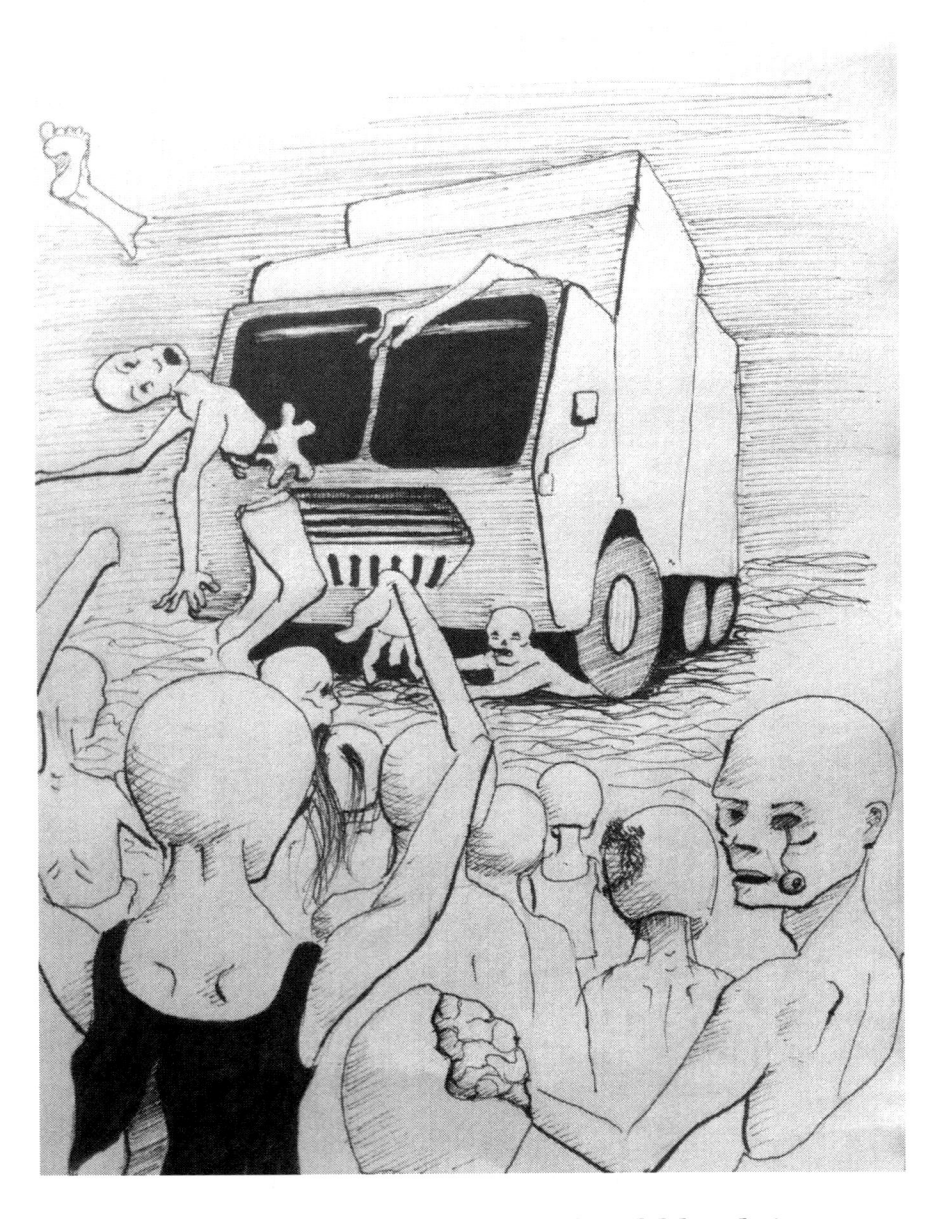

A truck doing exactly what it should be doing.

Bicycles and Motorcycles

Bicycles and Motorcycles are generally considered better than cars and trucks for evasion.

A motorcycle uses just a fraction of the fuel that a car does, and its small size lets it go where a car can't. A highway that is completely jammed with cars will probably have room for a motorcycle. When a motorcycle is no longer ride-able, it can be pushed fairly easily.

But motorcycles have a bad reputation on the roads for a reason: they're very dangerous. Motorcycles provide zero protection to their rider, and you can't run over a zombie with a motorcycle (unless you want to flip over and die). Also, although they need less fuel than a car, they still need it. When the fuel is gone, a motorcycle is actually even less useful than a car: at least a car can be used as a temporary shelter.

A bicycle looks lame, but it's probably the best transportation you can get in a zombie outbreak. It requires no fuel at all, it's even more maneuverable than the motorcycle, and best of all: it's nearly silent. Cars, trucks, and motorcycles all make loud engine noises that zombies can pick up for miles. This means that anyone using one is like the pied piper of zombies. Zombies will rarely notice a biker, and even if they do, the biker will quickly get out of range and leave the zombies in the dust.

If you're trying to get away from the zombies and are being as practical as possible, grab your bike and strap on your helmet. Just don't even think about using a bicycle to attack zombies.

Boats

Zombies cannot swim, so if you are in water deep enough that zombies won't be tugging at your keel, a boat is an invincible, moveable island. You can carry plenty of supplies and stay perfectly safe for days, weeks, even months at sea.

The trouble is, you will probably run out of supplies eventually. When this happens, you will either have to return to shore and face the zombies again, or forage on the open water. Or starve, but that's not a great idea.

If you plan to travel by boat, make carrying fresh water your top priority. Any healthy body of water can provide plenty to eat, but salt water isn't drinkable and fresh lake and pond water can contain nasty diseases. Boil water before drinking it, if you can.

Attacking zombies on a boat involves some practical problems. You can take potshots of zombies on the shore, but after a while, you're going to have to get out of your boat and explore the dry land to kill zombies inside houses or any that are far away from your boat. Also, zombies under the water are a definite possibility, but you can't actually attack them from your boat. Exterminating zombies underwater is a high-difficulty, high-danger operation that should not be tried by anyone but trained SCUBA divers.

Planes and Helicopters

Flying over zombies is easily the safest way to travel. When you're hundreds of feet up in the air, it's almost possible to forget that there even is a zombie outbreak!

But once again, the problem is fuel. Planes can't stay in the air forever, and refueling an airplane is not as simple as going to the local gas station with a can. Plus, planes are not easy to operate, and any amateur flying a plane is probably going to have to crash to get the plane back down on the ground. For obvious reasons, this is not a great idea.

Attacking zombies from a plane is nearly impossible. Attacking them from a helicopter can work, however. The noise of the chopper will draw zombies for miles, and the exterminators in the chopper will be completely invincible from the zombies. For the sake of conserving fuel however, it would probably be best to land the chopper on a tall building and kill the zombies from there, rather than hovering over the ground for hours at a time.

Skateboards and Other Toys

You might think that it's silly to use a skateboard or a pair of rollerblades to run away from, or attack, zombies, but they are actually quite useful in a city environment. Using these kinds of toys lets you move faster than a run, and they keep your hands free to use a weapon (which is something a bicycle can't really do). In rough terrain, these kinds of things are pointless, but in the setting in which they were supposed to work they can help.

Then again, there are toys that really are completely silly, like pogo sticks, unicycles, sleds, push-cars, and scooters. The zombies won't laugh at you if you use these. They'll just catch you and eat you.

On Foot

Going on foot will often end up being your only option, and it's not a bad one. Humans have been walking and running for thousands of years, and we've done just fine so far.

On foot, you can go absolutely anywhere if you have the food and time to get there. Clogged roads and rough terrain will never stop you. You will never run the risk of careening off a mountainside, or slamming into a wall. You won't run out of fuel and have to stop.

However, walking is the slowest way to travel, and it's tiring and difficult for people that are not used to it. A brisk walk around your neighborhood for an hour is nothing compared to 8 to 10 straight hours of cross-country hiking. You will be exhausted, but you will also get stronger as you go.

Avoid all-out running whenever possible: it saps energy a lot faster than walking does, and it leaves you vulnerable to ambushes and injuries. If you hurt yourself while on foot, there's really nothing anyone can do to help you.

Exterminating zombies on foot has to be done eventually. This is called "mop-up," and it's dangerous, just like anything is in a zombie outbreak. Stick with your group, lure zombies whenever you can, and watch your back.

What's the point of a vehicle without a destination? The next section discusses places to be in a zombie outbreak, and places NEVER to be.

DEFENSE

Where NOT to Go

There are several zombie "hot spots" that are the absolutely worst possible places to go to during an outbreak. These areas are the first places most people to go during a crises, or are the places where large groups of people generally tend to be anyway. They include:

-malls

-churches

-police stations

-government buildings

-hospitals

-department stores

Zombie outbreaks just about radiate from these locations. If you find that you are in one when an outbreak occurs, do your best to escape into open ground. If you can't, find an isolated area that you can hide in until you can escape later, such as an office with a window. Try to find a weapon, and sit tight: you're in a horror-movie scenario now. Good luck.

Where to Go

An apartment or office building can be terrific. If you shut down the elevators and destroy or barricade all the stairs, you can sit in the top floors of one of these buildings and never be bothered by a single zombie. You can enjoy hours of dropping stuff out the window and trying to bonk zombies on the head.

A small grocery store can provide good cover, and some defense from the steel shutters that will likely be used to lock the store up. And, obviously, the store can provide enough food to last a small group practically forever. Avoid stores with glass windows however, as these will put you on display for the zombies. Also, the steel shutters won't last forever against a hoard.

A prison can actually be an excellent hideout from zombies. They are built like fortresses and have tons of supplies, including weapons, ammo, food, and clothes. However, there is always the chance that a few dangerous criminals thought of these advantages too during an outbreak, and are holing up in the prison. Be careful, and sweep the building thoroughly before moving in.

In the end though, the best places to go are far, far away from where people normally gather. The best location of all is the Tundra, a northern, cold, wild climate. In the tundra, neither zombies nor raiders will likely bother you. You can easily create shelter and find enough food to last a lifetime. The tundra will let you see any zombies or humans approaching your location for miles, and the cold will often freeze zombies in their tracks for months on end, further reducing the likelihood that you will ever see one again.

Preparing an Area for Zombies

If you can't get to a good zombie-defense location, then grab some tools, 2X4's, and a big axe: you've got some work to do. It's time to turn your house into a fortress.

First, turn on all the faucets and taps in the house and collect as much water as possible. You will need this for drinking, if the water is turned off during the outbreak (it probably will be.)

Next, gather together all the supplies and weapons in the house and take inventory.

Move everything you can up to the second floor, and destroy the stairs. With the stairs gone, zombies will have no way to reach you.

If you cannot destroy the stairs, then barricade the windows and doors on the first floor and move up to the second floor. If you have no second floor, move onto the roof. The higher up you are, the safer you will be from zombies.

NEVER go into the basement. It may seem safe, but if zombies break into the basement then you have no way to escape.

If you have time, you may want to set up a perimeter using a ditch or fencing. This won't keep zombies away for long, but it can buy you time when you need it.

Above all, don't panic. You are smarter and more dangerous than a thousand zombies, if you stay calm.

An ideally fortified home. Notice the X-Rayed area showing the destroyed stairs. Even if zombies clear the trench and the humans keeping careful watch, they will have no way to access the second floor.

WORST CASE SCENARIOS

<u>What If I'm Out of Ammo and Surrounded?</u>

First, check the situation. There might be something you can use to help you escape. For example, you may be able to smash through the window of a house, or climb over a car or truck.

If no escape route can be made, then look for a hand-to-hand weapon if you don't already have one. Even a large stick can help push zombies out of the way, and since your goal now is survival, even that small advantage could save your life.

If you find a weapon or tool that can help you, then advance towards the part of the surrounding zombies that blocks the most open area you could break towards. Use your weapon to shove zombies out of your way and keep them away from grabbing you.

Do NOT try to dispatch enough zombies to escape. You will only be slowed down, and nearby zombies will catch you. No one will be there to see your dramatic death.

If you have no weapon to help, then tuck your arms in close to your body, lower your waist, and attempt to break through the lines. Thrash your body in tight, compact motions to break zombie's grips.

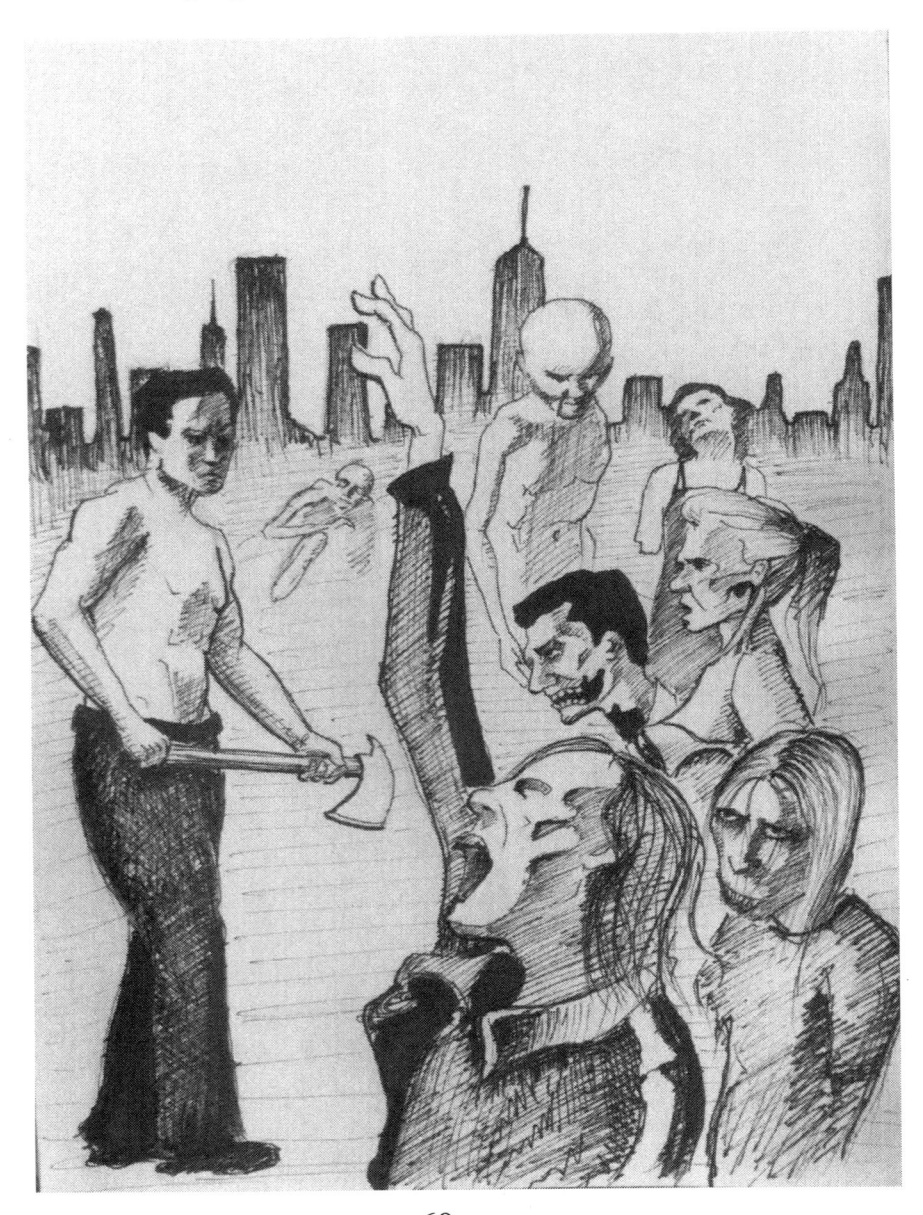

When surrounded by zombies, stay calm and check the situation. Then find a weapon or tool you can use to break past the line if there's no alternative.

What if I'm Injured, Alone, and Zombies Are Coming?

You're probably dead.

But just in case...

If your arms are fine but one or both of your legs are injured, drag yourself to the nearest tree. Use the trunk to support your body weight, and use your arms to pull yourself up to a branch. Try to climb as high as you can.

If your legs are fine but your arms are injured, break away into as much brush and cover as you can, and try to get to high ground so you can see zombies coming before they see you.

From a high vantage point, you will hopefully be able to spot and attract rescue.

If you can somehow find a weapon, you're way better off. Just try to avoid being seen.

What If Someone Is Bitten By a Zombie?

First, find out where the zombie bit them. If the wound is on the head, torso, or groin, then there's nothing you can do.

However, if the bite is on a limb, then there is an extremely small chance that a quick amputation will prevent the infection from spreading throughout the patient's body and turning them into a zombie.

Apply a tourniquet above the site of the bite wound, to prevent excessive blood loss. Then chop off the bitten limb. Don't screw this up.

The patient will hopefully pass out from the pain.

Seal the wound with fire or a red-hot brand.

After amputation, watch the patient carefully. If after 24 hours they are alive and have not turned into a zombie, then you have witnessed a miracle. If they die, get ready to kill a new zombie.

Conclusion

Now you should be ready to survive against zombies, and be able to kill any that stand in your way. Zombies may seem tough, but you have something they don't: knowledge. Use that against them, and you could beat 100 zombies (remember Sun Tzu?)

Share this manual with people you trust, so that you can survive together. Then, the human race might have a chance.

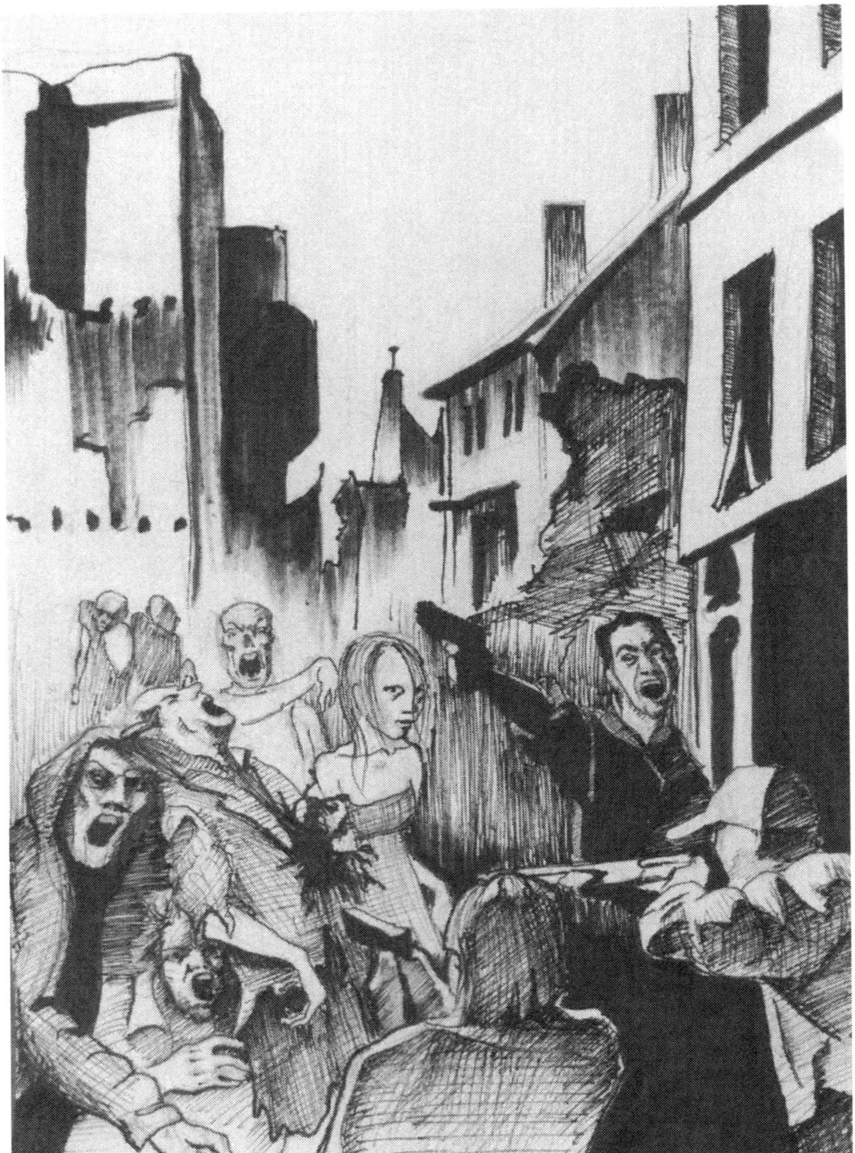

Printed in Great Britain
by Amazon